Those Fabulous '30s

by Gwen Hurlburt

Sweet Little Quilts to Brighten Your Day

CHITRA PUBLICATIONS
2 Public Avenue
Montrose, PA 18801-1220

Your Best Value in Quilting
www.QuiltTownUSA.com

Chitra Publications
2 Public Avenue
Montrose, Pennsylvania 18801-1220

First Printing: 2003

Library of Congress Cataloging-in-Publication Data

Hurlburt, Gwen.
  Those fabulous '30s : sweet little quilts to brighten your day / by Gwen Hurlburt.
     p. cm.
  ISBN 1-885588-48-8 (pbk.)
  1. Patchwork--Patterns. 2. Quilting--Patterns. 3. Patchwork quilts.
I. Title.
  TT835 .H86 2003
  746.46'041--dc21
                              2002015292

Edited by..Deborah Hearn and Virginia Jones
Design and Illustrations.................Diane M. Albeck-Grick
Cover Photography......................Guy Cali Associates, Inc.,
                                                     Clarks Summit, Pennsylvania
Inside Photography.......................Van Zandbergen Photography,
                                                     Brackney, Pennsylvania

Introduction

In the 1980s I made over 100 Teddy Bears, each with different designs and materials and in all sorts of sizes. One day my bear named "Bertha" said she was cold and asked me if I would make her a Bear's Paw quilt. To subdue the jealousy (and growling!) of the other bears, I made many, many more quilts all designed to match the size and pattern requests of each bear.

I also made many cloth dolls, each one different from the other, including more than three dozen Raggedy Anns and Andys. Each one had a quilt in a suitable size. As with most of my bears, I gave away most of my Anns and Andys.

Making small quilts enables me to try many different patterns and design ideas in a relatively small amount of time. I especially like traditional patterns and have found that most men

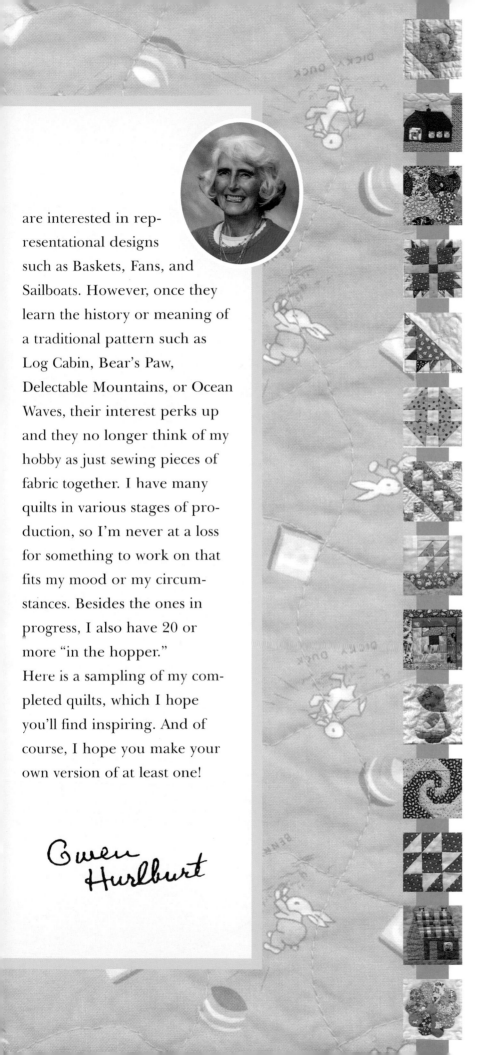

are interested in representational designs such as Baskets, Fans, and Sailboats. However, once they learn the history or meaning of a traditional pattern such as Log Cabin, Bear's Paw, Delectable Mountains, or Ocean Waves, their interest perks up and they no longer think of my hobby as just sewing pieces of fabric together. I have many quilts in various stages of production, so I'm never at a loss for something to work on that fits my mood or my circumstances. Besides the ones in progress, I also have 20 or more "in the hopper."

Here is a sampling of my completed quilts, which I hope you'll find inspiring. And of course, I hope you make your own version of at least one!

Gwen Hurlburt

Dedication

Dedicated to my husband Harry, "the spark of my life," who has a knack for coming up with a "choice comment" for each of my projects.

Table of Contents

Baskets w

A tisket a tasket, make charming little baskets! "Baskets with Flying Geese Border" is perfect for spring-time decorating or for year-round display.

Cutting

Fabrics will be precut for foundation piecing. All dimensions include a 1/4" seam allowance.

For each of 16 pairs of Basket blocks:

• Cut 1: 3 3/8" square, print, then cut it in half diagonally to yield 2 large triangles

• Cut 2: 1 5/8" squares, same print, then cut them in half diagonally to yield 4 small triangles

• Cut 2: 3/4" x 3 1/2" bias strips, same print

For the Foundation-pieced borders:

• Cut 120: 1 1/4" x 2" strips, assorted prints

• Cut 120: 1 3/4" squares, white, then cut them in half diagonally to yield 240 triangles

Also:

• Cut 16: 3 3/8" squares, white, then cut them in half diagonally to yield 32 large triangles

• Cut 64: 1 1/4" x 2 1/4" strips, white

• Cut 16: 2 3/8" squares, white, then cut them in half diagonally to yield 32 small triangles

• Cut 2: 1 1/2" x 32" strips, white

• Cut 4: 1 1/2" x 25 1/2" strips, white

• Cut 2: 1 1/2" x 18 7/8" strips, white

Quilt Size: 25" x 30"
Block Size: 3 1/4" square

Materials
• Assorted prints, each at least 2" square for the Flying Geese, and 8" square for the Baskets
• 1 yard white
• 27" x 32" piece of backing fabric
• 27" x 32" piece of thin batting
• Paper for the foundations

- Cut 3: 1 1/4" x 44" strips, white, for the binding
- Cut 2: 3 1/4" squares, white, then cut them in half diagonally to yield 4 corner triangles
- Cut 4: 5 7/8" squares, white, then cut them in quarters diagonally to yield 16 setting triangles. You will use 14.

Preparation

- Lightly trace the handle placement on the large white triangles.
- Press the long edges of the 3/4" x 3 1/2" bias strips in thirds.
- Trim 1/8" from each long edge.

Directions

For each pair of Basket blocks:

- Appliqué a prepared bias strip in place along the marked line to complete a Handle Unit. Make 2.

- Stitch the long edge of a handle unit to the long edge of a same print large triangle to complete a pieced square.

- Stitch same print small triangles to one end of two 1 1/4" x 2 1/4" white strips, as shown.

- Stitch them to the pieced square.

- Stitch a small white triangle to the remaining corner to complete a Basket block. Make 2.
- Make a total of 16 pairs.
- Lay out the blocks, on point, with white setting triangles along the edges and white corner triangles in the corners. Stitch them into diagonal rows and join the rows.

- Stitch the 1 1/2" x 18 7/8" white strips to the top and bottom of the quilt.

- Stitch 2 of the 1 1/2" x 25 1/2" white strips to the sides of the quilt.

For the Foundation-pieced borders:

Foundation patterns are full size and do not include a seam allowance.

- Trace the full-size pattern (on page 11) on the foundation paper, drawing 27 geese for the short borders and 37 geese for the long borders.
- Piece each foundation using assorted prints in the shaded sections and white in the unshaded sections. NOTE: *Trim the seam allowance to 1/8" after each piece is added.*

- Stitch the short Flying Geese borders to the top and bottom of the quilt.
- Stitch the long Flying Geese borders to the sides of the quilt.
- Measure the width of the quilt. Trim the remaining 1 1/2" x 25 1/2" white strips to that measurement. Stitch them to the top and bottom of the quilt.
- Measure the length of the quilt. Trim the 1 1/2" x 32" white strips to that measurement. Stitch them to the sides of the quilt.
- Gently remove the foundation paper.
- Finish the quilt according to the *General Directions*, using the 1 1/4" x 44" white strips for the binding.

Barnyard

All of the critters in *"Barnyard"* are happy to have a comfortable place to live, out of the cold, the wind, and the rain. You'll find that there's even a barn dance going on in one of the buildings. Enjoy collecting novelty prints to make your own version of this quilt.

Cutting

The patterns (page 9) are full size and do not include a turn-under allowance. Make templates for pattern pieces A through E. Trace around the templates on the right side of the fabric and add a 1/4" seam allowance when cutting the fabric pieces out. All other dimensions include a 1/4" seam allowance.

For each of 4 blocks:

- Cut 1: A, red print scrap
- Cut 1: 2 1/2" x 3 7/8" rectangle, red, for the side
- Cut 1: C, red
- Cut 1: B, red plaid
- Cut 1: D, same red plaid
- Cut 1: 2 1/4" x 5 1/4" bias rectangle, light plaid, for the silo
- Cut 1: E, dark print

NOTE: *The door and window size may vary according to the size of the motif you choose. Be sure to include a 1/4" turn-under allowance around the motif. See the Window Templates section in the* General Directions.

Quilt Size: 24" square
Block Size: 8 1/2" square

Materials

- 4 assorted red print scraps, each at least 5" square
- 4 red plaid scraps, each at least 6" square
- 4 light plaid scraps, each at least 3" x 6" for the silos
- 4 dark print scraps, each at least 3" square, for the silo tops
- Assorted novelty print scraps, each at least 2" square, for the border, barn windows and barn door
- 1/8 yard red
- 3/8 yard blue print, for the background
- 1/8 yard green print
- 1/2 yard white
- 26" square of backing fabric
- 26" square of thin batting
- Black permanent ink pen
- Template plastic (for fussy cutting pieces)

- Cut 1: door, centering the novelty print
- Cut 3 or 4: windows, centering the novelty print

Also:

- Cut 4: 7 1/2" x 9 1/2" rectangles, blue print
- Cut 4: 2 1/2" x 9 1/2" strips, green print
- 70: 1 1/2"-wide strips, ranging from 1 1/2" to 2 1/2" in length, centering the assorted novelty prints, for the pieced border
- Cut 2: 1 1/2" x 9" strips, white
- Cut 3: 1 1/2" x 18 1/2" strips, white
- Cut 2: 1 1/2" x 20 1/2" strips, white
- Cut 4: 1 1/2" x 27" strips, white
- Cut 3: 1 1/4" x 44" strips, white, for the binding

Directions

For each block:

- Stitch a 2 1/2" x 9 1/2" green print strip to a long side of a 7 1/2" x 9 1/2" blue print rectangle to form the background.
- Referring to the Placement Diagram, needleturn appliqué pieces to the background in the following order: 2 1/4" x 5 1/4" plaid bias rectangle (silo), 2 1/2" x 3 7/8" red rectangle

(side), red print A, red plaid B, red C, red plaid D, and dark print E.

- In the same manner, appliqué the door and windows to the barn to complete the block. Make 4. Trim them to 9" square.
- If desired, using the permanent ink pen, draw weathervanes emerging from the point of the cupolas (C's).

- Stitch a 1 1/2" x 9" white strip between 2 blocks to form a horizontal row. Make 2.

- Lay out the rows with a 1 1/2" x 18 1/2" white strip between them and at the top and bottom. Stitch them together.
- Stitch 1 1/2" x 20 1/2" white strips to the left and right sides of the quilt.
- Stitch 14 to 16 of the 1 1/2"-wide assorted novelty print rectangles together, end to end, to form a strip 20 1/2" long. Make sure the images are oriented in the proper direction. Make 2. Stitch them to the left and right sides of the quilt.
- Stitch fifteen to seventeen 1 1/2"-wide assorted print rectangles together, end to end, to form a strip 22 1/2" long. Make 2. Stitch them to the top and bottom of the quilt.
- Measure the length of the quilt. Trim 2 of the 1 1/2" x 27" white strips to that measurement and stitch them to opposite sides of the quilt.
- Measure the width of the quilt, including the borders. Trim the remaining 1 1/2" x 27" white strips to that measurement and stitch them to the remaining sides of the quilt.
- Finish the quilt according to the *General Directions*, using the 1 1/4" x 44" white strips, for the binding.

Apple Core

I pieced *"Apple Core"* while traveling through Colorado, New Mexico, and Texas in a motor home with my husband and 2 dogs. I cut the pieces ahead of time and did the handwork on the road. I thoroughly enjoy the process of hand piecing. If you haven't tried it, here's your opportunity to add this relaxing activity to your days.

Cutting

Pattern A is full size and does not include a seam allowance. Make a template for the pattern piece. Trace around the template on the wrong side of the fabric and add a 1/4" seam allowance. All other dimensions include a 1/4" seam allowance.

• Cut 169: A's, assorted prints

Also:

• Cut 1 1/4"-wide bias strips, blue print, to total at least 150" when joined for the binding

Directions

For hand piecing, stitch only on the traced line, being sure not to stitch into the seam allowance.

• Place 2 print A's, right sides together, as shown. Stitch them together easing the curves to fit.

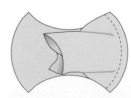

Quilt Size: 24 3/4" square

Materials

• Assorted prints, each at least 3" square
• Fat quarter (18" x 22") blue print for the binding
• 27" square of backing fabric
• 27" square of thin batting
• 3" square of template material

Hand piece this sweet one-patch design to showcase a wide variety of prints.

- Stitch 11 more A's to the first 2, alternating directions, to complete a Row A, as shown. Make 7.

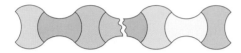

- In the same manner, stitch 13 A's together, as shown, to complete a Row B. Make 6.

- Lay out the Row A's alternately with the Row B's and stitch them together.
- Finish the quilt according to the *General Directions*, using the 1 1/4"-wide blue print bias strip for the binding.

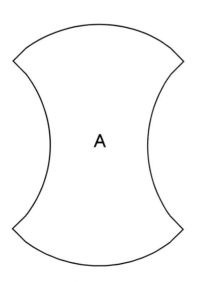

Full-Size Patterns for Barnyard

(The pattern begins on page 6.)

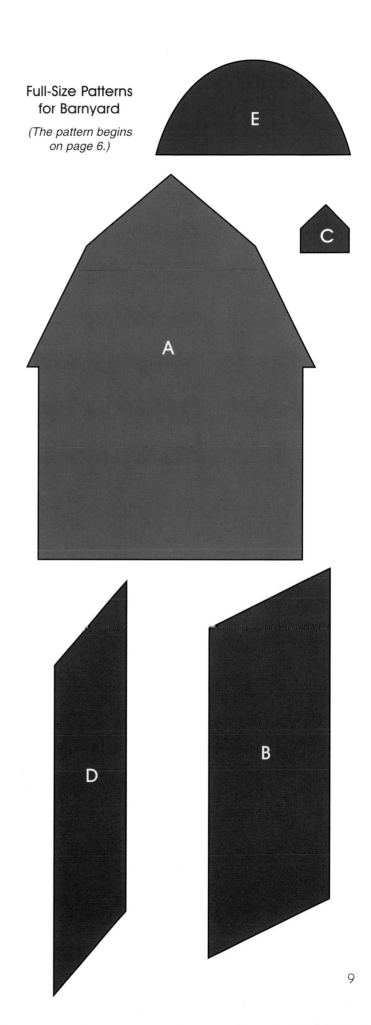

Bear's Paw

The official name of this quilt is **"Bear's Paw,"** but I think of it as Bear's Claws. Can you find the paw that has a hangnail? I like to imagine the bear was running and stubbed his toe on a rock or tree root.

Quilt Size: 23 1/2" square
Block Size: 3 1/2" square

Materials

- Assorted light and dark prints, each at least 4" square
- 1 1/8 yards white
- 1/8 yard blue print for the binding
- 26" square of backing fabric
- 26" square of thin batting

Cutting

Dimensions include a 1/4" seam allowance.

For each of 25 blocks:

- Cut 4: 1 1/2" squares, first dark print
- Cut 1: 1" square, second dark print
- Cut 4: 1" x 2" strips, light print

Also:

- Cut 73: 2 3/4" squares, assorted dark prints
- Cut 73: 2 3/4" squares, white
- Cut 104: 1" squares, white
- Cut 20: 1" x 4" strips, white
- Cut 4: 1" x 22" strips, white
- Cut 2: 2" x 22" strips, white
- Cut 2: 2" x 24" strips, white
- Cut 3: 1 1/4" x 44" strips, blue print, for the binding

Directions

- Draw diagonal lines from corner to corner on the wrong side of each 2 3/4" white square. Draw horizontal and vertical lines through the centers.
- Place a marked square on a 2 3/4" dark print square, right sides together. Stitch 1/4" away from both sides of the diagonal lines as shown. Make 73.

Go a little wild when mixing colors in this quilt.

**Partial Foundation
Pattern for Baskets with
Flying Geese Border**
(The pattern begins on page 4.)

• Cut the squares on the drawn lines to yield 584 pieced squares. You will use 580. Press the seam allowances toward the dark prints.

For each block:

• Lay out a 1 1/2" first dark print square, 4 pieced squares, and a 1" white square, as shown. Stitch them together to form a Paw Unit. Make 4.

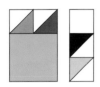

• Stitch the 1" second dark print square between two 1" x 2" light print strips to make a pieced strip.

• Lay out the pieced strip, 4 Paw Units, and the two 1" x 2" matching light print strips. Stitch the blocks and strips into 2 rows. Join the rows and the pieced strip to complete a Bear's Paw block. Make 25.

Assembly

• Lay out 5 Bear's Paw blocks with four 1" x 4" white strips, between them.

• Stitch the blocks and strips into a row. Make 5.

• Measure the length of the rows. Trim the 1" x 22" white strips to that measurement.

• Stitch the trimmed strips between the rows.

• Measure the width of the quilt. Trim the 2" x 22" white strips to that measurement and stitch them to opposite sides of the quilt.

• Measure the length of the quilt, including the borders. Trim the 2" x 24" white strips to that measurement and stitch them to the remaining sides of the quilt.

• Lay out 45 pieced squares, as shown, and stitch them together to form a pieced border. Make 4.

• Stitch pieced borders to 2 opposite sides of the quilt.

• Stitch a pieced border between two 1" white squares. Make 2.

• Stitch them to the remaining sides of the quilt.

• Finish the quilt according to the *General Directions*, using the 1 1/4" x 44" blue print strips for the binding.

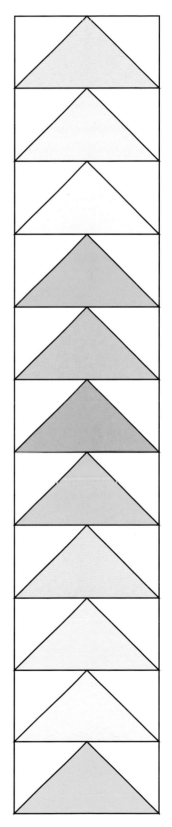

Extend the foundation to make 27 Geese for the short borders and 37 Geese for the long borders.

Delectabl Mountai

"Delectable Mountains" was inspired by a full-size quilt by Judy Knowles. Quilt historians believe the block's name came from John Bunyan's Pilgrim's Progress, an allegory filled with beautiful descriptive language.

Cutting

Dimensions include a 1/4" seam allowance.

- Cut 63: 3" squares, assorted prints
- Cut 15: 3 3/8" squares, assorted prints, then cut them in quarters diagonally to yield 60 medium triangles
- Cut 60: 1 3/8" squares, assorted prints, then cut them in half diagonally to yield 120 small triangles
- Cut 6: 4 1/8" squares, assorted prints, then cut them in quarters diagonally to yield 24 large triangles
- Cut 48: 1" x 1 1/2" strips, assorted prints
- Cut 63: 3" squares, white
- Cut 84: 1" squares, white
- Cut 30: 3 3/8" squares, white, then cut them in half diagonally to yield 60 triangles
- Cut 3: 1 1/4" x 36" strips, blue print, for the binding

Directions

- Draw diagonal lines from corner to corner on the wrong side of each 3"

Quilt Size: 22" square
Block Size: 2 1/2" square

Materials

- Assorted prints, each at least 4" square
- 1 yard white
- 1/8 yard blue print for the binding
- 24" square of backing fabric
- 24" square of thin batting

Your journey will be
pleasant and quick when you
speed-piece this sweet little quilt.

white square. Draw horizontal and vertical lines through the centers.

• Place a marked white square on a 3" print square, right sides together. Stitch 1/4" away from the diagonal lines on both sides. Make 63.

• Cut the squares on the drawn lincs to yicld 504 picccd squares. Press the seam allowances toward the print. Trim them to 1" square.

• Lay out 3 pieced squares facing left and 3 pieced squares facing right, as shown. Stitch them into pieced strips. Make 84 of each.

• Stitch a small print triangle to the end of each pieced strip, as shown. Make 60 of each. Set the remaining pieced strips aside.

• Stitch a pieced strip to a medium print triangle, as shown.

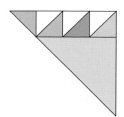

• Stitch a 1" white square to a mirror-image pieced strip and stitch it to the print triangle, as shown.

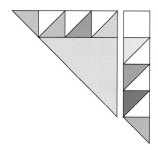

• Stitch a white triangle to the long edge of the unit to complete a Delectable Mountains Block. Make 60.

• Using the pieced strips you set aside, make 2 mirror-image pieced strips, stitching a 1" x 1 1/2" print strip to an end, as shown. Make 24 of each.

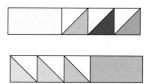

• Stitch a pieced strip to a large print triangle.

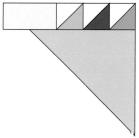

(continued on page 15)

Assembly
Diagram

Churn D Monkey

The block used in *"Churn Dash or Monkey Wrench"* conveniently has several titles according to Barbara Brackman's Encyclopedia of Pieced Quilt Patterns. I tell women it's Churn Dash, and I tell men it's Monkey Wrench. I think you'll enjoy stitching and naming your version of this traditional design.

Cutting

Dimensions include a 1/4" seam allowance.

For each of 25 blocks:

- Cut 2: 2 3/8" squares, print
- Cut 1: 1 1/4" x 10" strip, same print

Also:

- Cut 2: 1 1/4" squares, assorted prints
- Cut 50: 2 3/8" squares, white
- Cut 25: 1 1/4" x 10" strips, white
- Cut 27: 1 1/4" squares, white
- Cut 20: 1 1/4" x 4 1/4" strips, white
- Cut 6: 1 1/4" x 22 1/4" strips, white
- Cut 2: 1 1/4" x 23 3/4" strips, white
- Cut 2: 1 1/4" x 25 1/4" strips, white
- Cut 2: 1 1/4" x 26 3/4" strips, white
- Cut 3: 1 1/4" x 44" strips, blue print, for the binding

Directions

- Draw a diagonal line, from corner to corner, on the wrong side of each 2 3/8" white square.

Quilt Size: 26" square

Block Size: 3 3/4" square

Materials

- Assorted prints, each at least 5" x 10"
- 1 yard white
- 1/8 yard blue print for the binding
- 28" square of backing fabric
- 28" square of thin batting

ash or Wrench

Whatever you call it, this block is always in style!

Delectable Mountains
(continued from page 13)

For each block:

• Lay a marked white square on a 2 3/8" print square, right sides together, and stitch 1/4" away from the drawn line on both sides. Make 2.

• Cut the squares on the marked lines to yield 4 pieced squares.
• Stitch the 1 1/4" x 10" matching print strip to a 1 1/4" x 10" white strip, along their length.
• Cut seven 1 1/4" slices from the pieced strip. Set aside 3 of them for the border.

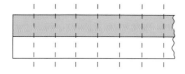

• Lay out 4 slices, 4 matching pieced squares, and a 1 1/4" white square in 3 rows of 3, as shown.

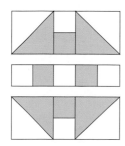

• Stitch the slices and squares into rows and join the rows to complete a Churn Dash block. Make 25.
• Lay out 5 blocks alternately with four 1 1/4" x 4 1/4" white strips. Stitch them into a row. Make 5.
• Lay out the rows alternately with six 1 1/4" x 22 1/4" white strips, and stitch them together.
• Stitch 1 1/4" x 23 3/4" white strips to the long sides of the quilt.
• Stitch 15 of the set-aside 1 1/4" slices and one 1 1/4" print square together, end to end, to form a pieced border that begins and ends with a print square. Make 2.

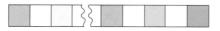

• Stitch them to opposite sides of the quilt.
• Stitch 16 of the set-aside 1 1/4" slices and one 1 1/4" white square together to make a long pieced border that begins and ends with a white square. Make 2.
• Stitch them to the remaining sides of the quilt. You will have 13 slices left over for use in another project.
• Stitch the 1 1/4" x 25 1/4" white strips to opposite sides of the quilt.
• Stitch the 1 1/4" x 26 3/4" white strips to the remaining sides of the quilt.
• Finish the quilt according to the *General Directions*, using the 1 1/4" x 44" blue print strips for the binding.

• Stitch a 1" white square to a mirror-image pieced strip and stitch it to the print triangle.

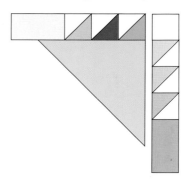

• Trim the excess from the 1" x 1 1/2" print strips even with the long edge of the triangle to complete a setting block. Make 24.

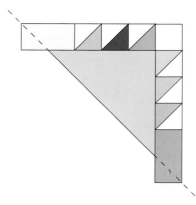

• Referring to the Assembly Diagram on page 13, lay out the blocks on point with the setting blocks along the edges. Stitch them into diagonal rows. One corner of the setting blocks will extend beyond the edge of the remaining blocks in the row. Trim them even with the remainder of the row, and then join the rows.
• Finish the quilt according to the *General Directions*, using the 1 1/4" x 36" blue print strips for the binding.

Jacob's Ladder

The white squares in *"Jacob's Ladder"* represent steps ascending from earth to heaven.

Quilt Size: 25" square
Block Size: 3" square

Materials

- Fat quarter (18" x 22") each of 6 prints in pink, orange, yellow, blue, green, and purple NOTE: *For a more scrappy look, substitute 2 fat eighths (11" x 18") for each fat quarter.*
- 1 1/4 yards white
- 1/8 yard blue print for the binding
- 27" square of backing fabric
- 27" square of thin batting

Cutting

Dimensions include a 1/4" seam allowance.

For each of 36 blocks, including 4 yellow, 7 purple, 6 pink, 5 orange, 7 green and 7 blue:

- Cut 1: 1" x 15" strip, print
- Cut 2: 1 7/8" squares, same print

Also:

- Cut 30: 2 3/4" squares, assorted prints, then cut them in quarters diagonally to yield 120 triangles NOTE: *A pair of triangles will need to match each leftover Four Patch Unit. You might want to cut these later.*
- Cut 36: 1" x 15" strips, white
- Cut 72: 1 7/8" squares, white
- Cut 2: 1 3/8" x 18 1/2" strips, white
- Cut 2: 1 3/8" x 20 1/4" strips, white
- Cut 4: 1 3/4" x 28" strips, white
- Cut 3: 1 1/4" x 44" strips, blue print, for the binding

Directions

For each block:

- Stitch the 1" x 15" print strip to a 1" x 15" white strip, along their length.
- Cut fourteen 1" slices from the pieced strip.

This heavenly quilt is quick and easy to piece.

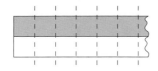

- Stitch 2 slices together to form a Four Patch Unit. Make 7.

- Draw a diagonal line from corner to corner on the wrong side of each 1 7/8" white square.
- Place a marked white square on a 1 7/8" print square, right sides together. Stitch 1/4" away from the diagonal line on both sides. Make 2 with matching print squares.

- Cut the squares on the drawn lines to yield 4 pieced squares. Press the seam allowances toward the print.
- Lay out 5 of the Four Patch Units and the 4 pieced squares, as shown. Stitch them into rows and join the rows to complete a Jacob's Ladder Block. Make 36. Set aside the left-over Four Patch Units for use in the border.

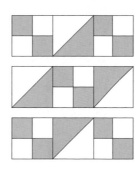

- Referring to the quilt photo for color placement, lay out the blocks in 6 rows of 6. Stitch them into rows and join the rows.
- Stitch the 1 3/8" x 18 1/2" white strips to opposite sides of the quilt.
- Stitch the 1 3/8" x 20 1/4" white strips to the remaining sides of the quilt.
- Stitch matching triangles to opposite sides of a left-over Four Patch Unit to form a Border Unit. Make 56.
- Stitch matching triangles to adjoining sides of a leftover Four Patch Unit to form a Corner Unit. Make 4. You will have 12 Four Patch units left over for use in another project.

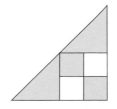

- Stitch 14 Border Units and a Corner Unit together to complete a pieced border. Make 4.

- Center and stitch pieced borders to opposite sides of the quilt top, starting, stopping, and backstitching 1/4" from the raw edges.
- Center and stitch pieced borders to the remaining sides of the quilt in the same manner.
- Stitch the corner seams.

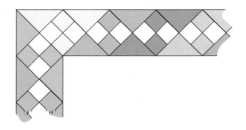

- Measure the length of the quilt. Trim 2 of the 1 3/4" x 28" white strips to that measurement and stitch them to opposite sides of the quilt.
- Measure the width of the quilt, including the borders. Trim the remaining 1 3/4" x 28" white strips to that measurement and stitch them to the remaining sides of the quilt.
- Finish the quilt according to the *General Directions*, using the 1 1/4" x 44" blue print strips for the binding.

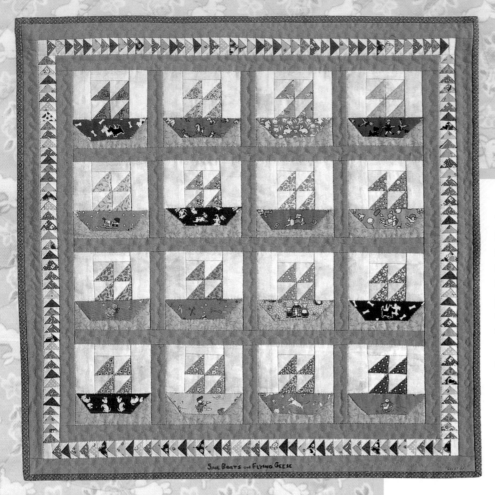

Sailboats

"*Sailboats*" *tells a story for me. It was a beautiful sunny day and many families decided to go sailing on the lake. Each owner had personalized their own boat so that it didn't look like all the others. The poor geese were circling around their lake wondering what happened and if they would ever find a place to land.*

Cutting

Dimensions include a 1/4" seam allowance.

For each of 16 blocks:

- Cut 2: 1 7/8" squares, first print
- Cut 1: 1 1/2" x 4 1/2" strip, second print

For the foundation-pieced borders:

- Cut 168: 1" x 1 1/2" strips, assorted prints, for the shaded sections
- Cut 168: 1 1/2" squares, cloud print, then cut them in half diagonally to yield 336 triangles, for the unshaded sections

Also:

- Cut 32: 1 1/2" x 3" strips, cloud print
- Cut 16: 1" x 2 1/2" strips, cloud print
- Cut 4: 1" x 1 1/2" strips, cloud print
- Cut 32: 1 7/8" squares, cloud print
- Cut 16: 1" x 4 1/2" strips, light blue print
- Cut 32: 1 1/2" squares, light blue print

Quilt Size: 24" square

Block Size: 4" square

Materials

- Assorted prints, 2" square and 2" x 5"
- 1/3 yard cloud print
- 1/8 yard light blue print for the water
- 1/2 yard medium blue
- 1/6 yard dark blue print for the binding
- 26" square of backing fabric
- 26" square of thin batting
- Paper for the foundations

You don't have to wait
for a fine, sunny day to
enjoy sewing these sloops.

- Cut 12: 1 1/4" x 4 1/2" strips, medium blue, for the sashing
- Cut 3: 1 1/4" x 20" strips, medium blue, for the sashing
- Cut 2: 1 3/8" x 23" strips, medium blue, for the inner border
- Cut 2: 1 3/8" x 20" strips, medium blue, for the inner border
- Cut 2: 1 1/2" x 22 1/2" strips, medium blue, for the outer border
- Cut 2: 1 1/2" x 24 1/2" strips, medium blue, for the outer border
- Cut 3: 1 1/4" x 44" strips, dark blue print, for the binding

Directions

- Draw a diagonal line from corner to corner on the wrong side of each 1 7/8" cloud print square.

For each Sailboat block:

- Place a marked cloud print square on a 1 7/8" first print square, right sides together, and stitch 1/4" away from the diagonal line on both sides. Make 2.

- Cut the squares on the marked lines to yield 4 pieced squares.
- Lay out the 4 pieced squares in 2 rows of 2, as shown, and stitch

them together.

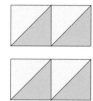

- Stitch a 1" x 2 1/2" cloud print strip to the top of the pieced squares.

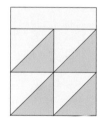

- Stitch 1 1/2" x 3" cloud print strips to the left and right sides to make the sail section. Set it aside.

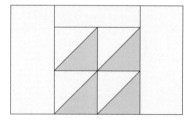

- Draw a diagonal line from corner to corner on the wrong side of each 1 1/2" light blue print square.
- Place marked squares on opposite ends of the 1 1/2" x 4 1/2" second print strip, as shown, and stitch on the drawn lines.

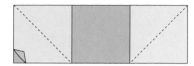

- Press the squares toward the corners, aligning the edges. Trim the seam allowances to 1/4" to complete the boat section.
- Stitch the sail section to the boat section.
- Stitch a 1" x 4 1/2" light blue print strip to the bottom to complete a Sailboat block. Make 16.

Assembly

- Lay out 4 blocks with 1 1/4" x 4 1/2" medium blue strips between them. Stitch them into a row. Make 4.
- Measure the length of the rows. Trim the 1 1/4" x 20" medium blue strips to that measurement and stitch them between the rows.
- Measure the length of the quilt. Trim the 1 3/8" x 20" medium blue strips to that measurement and stitch them to the sides of the quilt.
- Measure the width of the quilt, including the borders. Trim the 1 3/8" x 23" medium blue strips to that measurement and stitch them to the top and bottom of the quilt.

For the Foundation-pieced borders:

Foundation patterns are full size and
(continued on page 21)

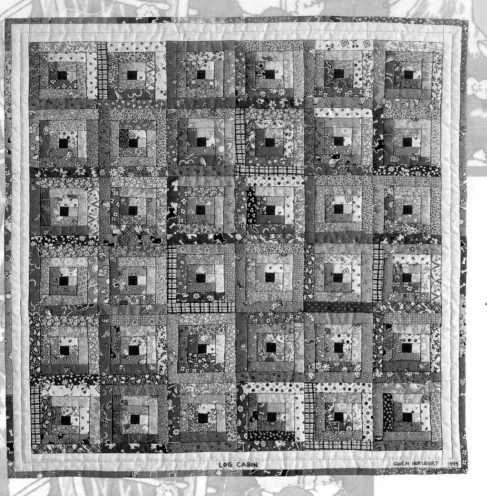

Log Cabin

I opted for traditional red centers in the blocks of my **"Log Cabin"** to signify a bright, cheery fire inside the hearth. Use your leftover scraps to construct the logs. Isn't it nice to turn leftovers into pretty quilts?

Quilt Size: 23" square
Block Size: 3 1/2" square

Materials

- Assorted medium prints in green, blue, and purple, each at least 1" wide and up to 4" long
- Assorted light prints in white, yellow, orange, and green, at least 1" wide and up to 3 1/2" long
- Fat eighth (11" x 18") red
- 1/4 yard white
- 25" square of backing fabric
- 25" square of thin batting
- Paper for the foundations

Cutting

Fabric for foundation piecing will be cut as you stitch the blocks. Each piece must be at least 1/4" larger on all sides than the section it will cover. Refer to the General Directions as needed. All other dimensions include a 1/4" seam allowance.

- Cut 2: 1 1/2" x 21 1/2" strips, white
- Cut 2: 1 1/2" x 23 1/2" strips, white
- Cut 15 to 20: 1 1/4"-wide assorted medium print strips, in lengths ranging from 4" to 8" and join them end to end to form a pieced strip at least 100" in length for the binding

Directions

Foundation patterns are full size and do not include a seam allowance. Follow the foundation-piecing instructions in the General Directions to piece the blocks.

- Trace the full-size pattern 36 times on the foundation material, transferring all lines and numbers. Cut each one out on the outer lines.
- Piece the foundations in numerical

Color contrasts don't have to be sharp to be effective.

order using the following fabrics in these positions:

1 - red

2, 3 - assorted light prints

4, 5 - assorted medium prints

6, 7 - assorted light prints

8, 9 - assorted medium prints

10, 11 - assorted light prints

12, 13 - assorted medium prints

• Trim the fabrics 1/4" beyond the edges of each foundation.

• Referring to the quilt photo for block orientation, lay out the blocks in 6 rows of 6. Stitch them into rows and join the rows.

• Stitch the 1 1/2" x 21 1/2" white strips to opposite sides of the quilt.

• Stitch the 1 1/2" x 23 1/2" white strips to the remaining sides of the quilt.

• Gently remove the paper foundations.

• Finish the quilt according to the *General Directions*, using the 1 1/4"-wide pieced strip for the binding.

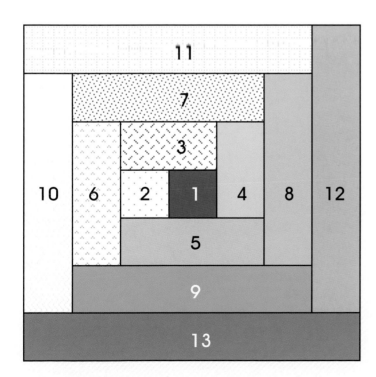

Sailboats

(continued from page 19)

do not include a seam allowance.

• Trace the full-size patterns (page 23) on the foundation paper, extending the foundation to make 40 geese for the short borders and 44 geese for the long borders. Follow the foundation piecing instructions in the *General Directions* to piece the borders.

• Piece each foundation using the following fabrics in these positions NOTE: *Trim the seam allowance to 1/8" after each piece is added.*

Shaded sections - assorted print triangles

Unshaded sections - cloud print triangles

• Trim the fabrics 1/4" beyond the edges of each foundation.

• Stitch the short borders to the sides of the quilt.

• Stitch a 1" x 1 1/2" cloud print strip to the beginning and end of the long borders.

• Stitch them to the top and bottom of the quilt.

• Stitch the 1 1/2" x 22 1/2" medium blue strips to the sides of the quilt.

• Stitch the 1 1/2" x 24 1/2" medium blue strips to the top and bottom of the quilt.

• Gently remove the paper foundations.

• Finish the quilt according to the *General Directions*, using the 1 1/4" x 44" dark blue print strips for the binding.

I made *"Sunbonnet Sue"* to display with my collection of cloth dolls. Each Sue is dressed differently as they model a variety of my scraps. You'll enjoy selecting favorite fabrics for your own version of this little quilt.

Cutting

The appliqué patterns below are full size and do not include a turn-under allowance. Make templates for the pattern pieces. Trace around the templates on the right side of the fabrics and add a 1/8" to 3/16" turn-under allowance when cutting the fabric pieces out. All other dimensions include a 1/4" seam allowance.

For each of 12 blocks:

• Cut 1 each: A, C, and F, assorted prints

• Cut 1 each: B and E, one print

Also:

• Cut 50: 2" squares, assorted prints

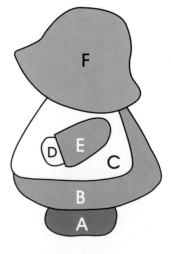

Quilt Size: 12" x 15"
Block Size: 2 1/2" square

Materials

• Assorted prints, 1 1/4" square to 4" square

• 4" square of muslin

• 1/8 yard white print

• 1/8 yard gray print

• 1/8 yard purple print

• 14" x 17" piece of backing fabric

• 14" x 17" piece of thin batting

net
ue

Indulge your fashion sense while choosing fabrics for this very chic little quilt.

Partial Foundation Pattern for Sailboats

(The pattern begins on page 18.)

- Cut 12: D, muslin
- Cut 12: 3 1/2" squares, white print
- Cut 8: 1" x 3" strips, gray print
- Cut 3: 1" x 9" strips, gray print
- Cut 2: 1 1/4" x 9" strips, gray print
- Cut 2: 1 1/4" x 13 1/2" strips, gray print
- Cut 2: 1 1/4" x 44" strips, purple print, for the binding

Directions

- Lightly mark the placement of a Sunbonnet Sue centered on the right side of the 3 1/2" white print squares.

- Needleturn appliqué the pieces for one block in alphabetical order on a 3 1/2" white print square. Make 12.
- Trim the blocks to 3" square.
- Lay out 3 blocks with 1" x 3" gray print strips between them. Stitch them into a row. Make 4.
- Lay out the rows with 1" x 9" gray print strips between them. Stitch

them together.
- Stitch the 1 1/4" x 9" gray print strips to the top and bottom of the quilt.
- Stitch the 1 1/4" x 13 1/2" gray print strips to the sides of the quilt.
- Draw a diagonal line from corner to corner on the wrong side of 25 of the 2" assorted print squares.
- Place a marked square on an unmarked 2" print square, right sides together. Stitch 1/4" away from the drawn line on both sides. Make 25.
- Cut the squares on the drawn lines to yield 50 pieced squares. Trim them to 1 1/2" square.
- Lay out 13 of the pieced squares, as shown. Stitch them together to form a long pieced border. Make 2.

- Stitch them to the sides of the quilt.
- In the same manner, stitch 12 pieced squares together to form a short pieced border. Make 2.
- Stitch them to the top and bottom of the quilt.
- Finish the quilt according to the *General Directions*, using the 1 1/4" x 44" purple print strips for the binding.

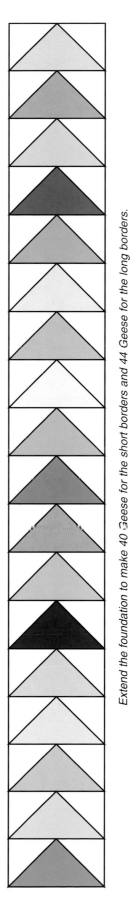

Extend the foundation to make 40 Geese for the short borders and 44 Geese for the long borders.

SNAIL'S TRAIL

Snail's Trail

Aim for good contrast in each block when you select fabric for your version of this quilt. *"Snail's Trail"* produces swirls of bright colors for pleasant eye stimulation. It may look complicated, but it's not with easy foundation piecing.

Cutting

Fabric for foundation piecing will be cut as you stitch the blocks. Each piece must be at least 1/2" larger on all sides than the section it will cover. Refer to the General Directions *as needed. All other dimensions include a 1/4" seam allowance.*

For the center of each of the 20 blocks:

- Cut 2: 1" squares, dark print
- Cut 2: 1" squares, medium print

Also:

- Cut 4: 1" x 23" strips, purple print
- Cut 4: 1 1/2" x 24" strips, white
- Cut 4: 1" x 26" strips, red print
- Cut 3: 1 1/4" x 44" strips, red print, for the binding

Quilt Size: 20" x 24"
Block Size: 4" square

Materials

- 20 assorted dark prints, each at least 6" square
- 20 assorted medium prints, each at least 6" square
- 1/8 yard purple print
- 1/4 yard white
- 1/4 yard red print
- 22" x 26" piece of backing fabric
- 22" x 26" piece of thin batting
- Paper for the foundations

Directions

- Lay out four 1" squares for the center of a block, as shown. Stitch them together to form a Four Patch Unit. Make 20.

For the Snail's Trail blocks:

The foundation pattern is full size and does not include a seam allowance. Follow the foundation-piecing instructions in the General Directions *to piece*

Foundation piecing tames the points and small pieces in these blocks.

the blocks.

- Trace the full-size pattern 20 times on the foundation paper, transferring all lines and numbers. Cut each one out on the outer lines. NOTE: *I reversed the foundation for 3 of my blocks.*
- Piece each foundation in numerical order using the following fabrics in these positions:

1 - Place the Four Patch Units in Position 1 on the unmarked side of the foundation, as shown, with the darker squares in the upper left and lower right corners, as shown. NOTE: *If you reversed the foundation for any blocks, you still place the Four Patch Units in the same position.*

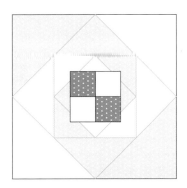

2, 3 - same dark print

4, 5, 6, 7 - same medium print

8, 9 - same dark print

10, 11 - same medium print

12, 13, 14, 15 - same dark print

16, 17 - same medium print

- Trim the fabrics 1/4" beyond the edges of each foundation.
- Referring to the quilt photo, lay out the blocks in 5 rows of 4.
- Stitch them into rows. Join the rows.
- Measure the length of the quilt. Trim 2 of the 1" x 23" purple print strips to that measurement. Stitch them to the long sides of the quilt.
- Measure the width of the quilt, including the borders. Trim the remaining 1" x 23" purple print strips to that measurement. Stitch them to the remaining sides of the quilt.
- In the same manner, trim 2 of the 1 1/2" x 24" white strips to fit the quilt's length and stitch them to the long sides of the quilt.
- Trim the remaining 1 1/2" x 24" white strips to fit the quilt's width and stitch them to the remaining sides of the quilt.
- Trim 2 of the 1" x 26" red print strips to fit the quilt's length and stitch them to the long sides of the quilt.
- Trim the remaining 1" x 26" red print strips to fit the quilt's width and stitch them to the remaining sides of the quilt.
- Gently remove the paper foundations.
- Finish the quilt according to the *General Directions*, using the 1 1/4" x 44" red print strips for the binding.

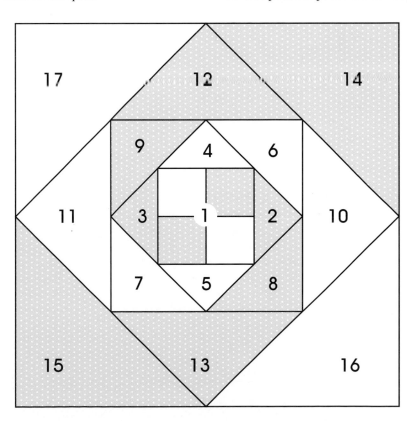

Tennessee Puzzle

"Tennessee Puzzle" was inspired by a full-sized quilt made by Jill Reber and Lynn Johnson. I used almost all light to medium fabrics except for the one black print that gives the quilt a little zip!

Cutting

Dimensions include a 1/4" seam allowance.

For each of 18 white-background blocks:

- Cut 1: 3 3/4" square, print

For each of 18 print-background blocks:

- Cut 1: 3 3/4" square, print
- Cut 3: 1 1/2" squares, same print

Also:

- Cut 84: 1 1/2" squares, assorted prints
- Cut 36: 3 3/4" squares, white
- Cut 54: 1 1/2" squares, white
- Cut 2: 1 1/2" x 18 1/2" strips, white
- Cut 2: 1 1/2" x 20 1/2" strips, white
- Cut 2: 1 3/4" x 22 1/2" strips, white
- Cut 2: 1 3/4" x 25" strips, white
- Cut 3: 1 1/4" x 44" strips, pink print, for the binding

Directions

- Draw diagonal lines from corner to corner on the wrong side of each 3 3/4"

Quilt Size: 25" square

Block Size: 3" square

Materials

- Assorted prints, 4" square and 6" square
- 1 yard white
- 1/8 yard pink print for the binding
- 27" square of backing fabric
- 27" square of thin batting

white square. Draw horizontal and vertical lines through the centers.

For each white-background block:

• Place a marked white square on a 3 3/4" print square, right sides together. Stitch 1/4" away from both sides of the diagonal lines, as shown.

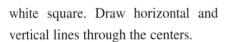

• Cut the square on the drawn lines to yield 8 pieced squares. You will use 6. Press the seam allowances toward the print.

• Lay out 6 pieced squares with three 1 1/2" white squares, as shown.

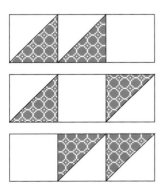

• Stitch them into rows and join the rows to complete a white-background block. Make 18.

For each print-background block:

• Make a print background block in the same manner using the remaining 3 3/4" white and 3 3/4" print squares, three 1 1/2" matching print squares instead of the white squares, and laying out the pieces, as shown.

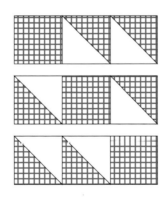

• Stitch them into rows and join the rows to complete the block. Make 18.

Assembly

• Referring to the quilt photo for block orientation, lay them out, alternating white-background blocks with print-background blocks, in 6 rows of 6. Stitch them into rows and join the rows.

• Stitch the 1 1/2" x 18 1/2" white strips to opposite sides of the quilt.

• Stitch the 1 1/2" x 20 1/2" white strips to the remaining sides of the quilt.

• Stitch twenty 1 1/2" assorted print squares together to form a short pieced border. Make 2.

• Stitch them to opposite sides of the quilt.

• Stitch twenty-two 1 1/2" assorted print squares together to form a long pieced border. Make 2. Stitch them to the remaining sides of the quilt.

• Stitch the 1 3/4" x 22 1/2" white strips to opposite sides of the quilt.

• Stitch the 1 3/4" x 25" white strips to the remaining sides of the quilt.

• Finish the quilt according to the *General Directions*, using the 1 1/4" x 44" pink print strips for the binding

Housing Tract #1

While working with 1930s prints, I thought some of the printed people might like to have a home of their own, and the result was *"Housing Tract #1."* You'll notice that the construction company built all the houses in the same size and style, but the owners managed to individualize them anyway.

Cutting

Patterns A and B are full size and do not include a 1/4" seam allowance. The directions provide for rotary cutting the remaining pieces, but you may prefer to make see-through templates to fussy-cut images from the fabrics. Make templates for pattern pieces A and B and, if desired, for the doors, windows and border rectangles. See the Window Templates section in the General Directions. Trace around the templates on the right side of the fabric and add a 1/4" seam allowance when cutting the pieces out. All other dimensions include a 1/4" seam allowance.

For each of 9 blocks:

- Cut 1: A, print
- Cut 1: B, second print or plaid
- Cut 1: 2 1/4" x 3 1/2" rectangle, third print, for the house front
- Cut 1: 1 1/4" x 2" rectangle, fourth print, for the door
- Cut 1: 1 1/4" square, novelty print, for the window

Also:

- Cut 18: 3/4" x 1" rectangles, red plaid

Quilt Size: 24 1/4" square
Block Size: 5 1/4" square

Materials

- Assorted prints and plaids, each at least 6" square
- Assorted novelty prints, each at least 2" square, for the pieced border and windows
- 3/8 yard blue print for the background
- 1/8 yard green print for the grass
- 3/4 yard white
- 27" square of backing fabric
- 27" square of thin batting

- Cut 9: 5 1/2" x 6" rectangles, blue print
- Cut 9: 1 1/2" x 6" green print strips
- Cut 62: 1 1/2"-wide rectangles ranging from 1 3/4" to 2 1/2" in length, assorted novelty prints NOTE: *Some designs should be placed vertically for the side borders and others horizontally for the top and bottom borders.*
- Cut 6: 1 1/2" x 5 3/4" strips, white
- Cut 4: 1 1/2" x 18 1/4" strips, white
- Cut 2: 1 1/2" x 20 1/4" strips, white
- Cut 4: 1 1/2" x 26" strips, white
- Cut 3: 1 1/4" x 44" strips, white, for the binding

Directions

For each block:

- Referring to the quilt photo, needleturn appliqué the pieces for one house to a 5 1/2" x 6" blue print rectangle in the following order: print A (house side), 2 1/4" x 3 1/2" third print

rectangle (house front), two 3/4" x 1" red plaid rectangles (chimneys), and second print or plaid B (roof). NOTE: *Align the bottom edges but don't turn-under the seam allowance on these edges.*

- Needleturn appliqué the 1 1/4" x 2" fourth print rectangle (door) and 1 1/4" novelty print square (window) to the house front.
- Stitch the 1 1/2" x 6" green print strip to the bottom of the house to complete a block. Make 9. Trim them to 5 3/4" square.

Assembly

- Lay out 3 blocks in a horizontal row with 1 1/2" x 5 3/4" white strips between them. Stitch them into a row. Make 3.
- Lay out the rows with 1 1/2" x 18 1/4" white strips between them and at the top and bottom of the quilt. Stitch them together.
- Stitch 1 1/2" x 20 1/4" white

strips to the left and right sides of the quilt.

- Stitch 13 to 15 of the 1 1/2"-wide assorted novelty print rectangles together, end to end, to form a strip 20 1/4" long. Make 2. Stitch them to the left and right sides of the quilt.
- In the same manner, stitch 14 to 16 of the 1 1/2"-wide assorted novelty print rectangles together, end to end, to form a strip 22 1/4" long. Make 2. Stitch them to the top and bottom of the quilt.
- Measure the length of the quilt. Trim 2 of the 1 1/2" x 26" white strips to that measurement and stitch them to the sides of the quilt.
- Measure the width of the quilt, including the borders. Trim the remaining 1 1/2" x 26" white strips to that measurement and stitch them to the top and bottom of the quilt.
- Finish the quilt according to the *General Directions*, using the 1 1/4" x 44" white strips for the binding.

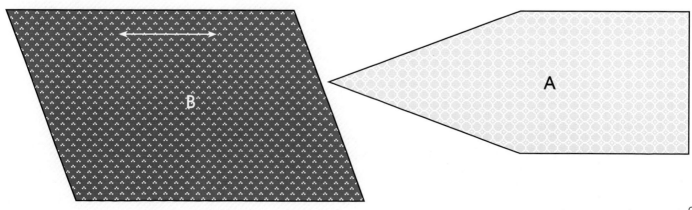

Dresden Plate

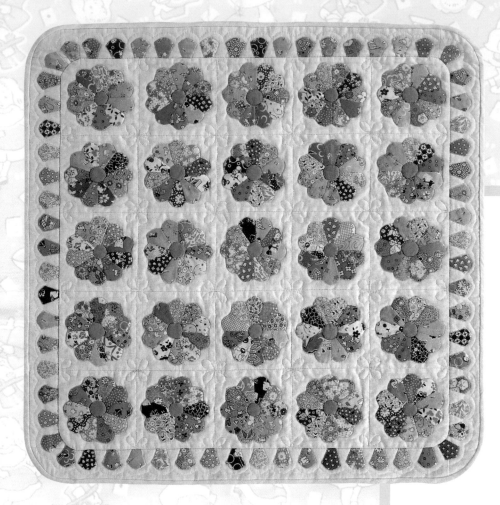

"Dresden Plate" is a well-traveled quilt. I cut the pieces ahead of time and took them with me on several trips over a number of years. They spent a few weeks in Montana and Wyoming and an entire summer in Alaska. In order to mimic the flat appearance of vintage quilts, I divided a low-loft batting so that the piece I used was only one-third of the usual thickness.

Cutting

Pattern A is full size and includes a 1/4" seam allowance. Pattern B is full size and does not include a seam allowance. Make a template for each pattern piece. Trace around template A on the right side of the fabric and cut the fabric pieces out on the lines. Trace around template B on the right side of the fabric and add a 1/8" to 3/16" turn-under allowance when cutting the fabric pieces out. All other dimensions include a 1/4" seam allowance.

- Cut 314: A, assorted prints
- Cut 25: B, orange

Quilt Size: 23" square
Block Size: 4" square

Materials

- Assorted prints, each at least 2" square
- 1/8 yard orange
- 1 1/4 yards white
- 25" square of backing fabric
- 25" square of thin batting

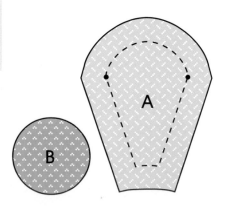

- Cut 25: 5" squares, white
- Cut 2: 3 1/2" x 25 1/2" strips, white
- Cut 2: 3 1/2" x 19" strips, white
- Cut 3: 1 1/4" x 44" bias strips, white, for the binding

Directions

For each block:

- Stitch 2 print A's together, stopping, and backstitching at the dot, as shown. Make 5.

- Stitch the pairs together in the same manner to complete a plate.

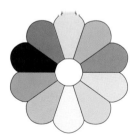

- Center the plate on a 5" white square, right sides up, and needleturn appliqué the outer edge of the plate in place.
- Needleturn appliqué an orange circle (B) over the center of the plate, covering the raw edges.
- Trim the block to 4 1/2" square. Make 25.

Assembly

- Lay out the blocks in 5 rows of 5. Stitch them into rows and join the rows.
- Trim each corner of the quilt top in a gradual curve.

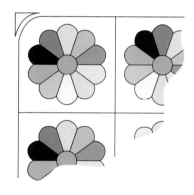

- Press the edges of the quilt top 1/4" toward the wrong side.
- Stitch the 3 1/2" x 19" white strips to the 3 1/2" x 25 1/2" white strips to make a border frame, as shown.

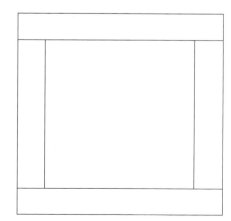

- Center the quilt top on the border

frame, right side up. Pin them together in a few places.

- Place a print A on the border in each corner, tucking the 1/4" seam allowance under the edge of the quilt top. Pin them to the border. Evenly space and pin 15 print A's along each side of the quilt, tucking the seam allowances under the quilt top.

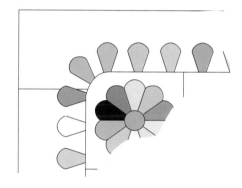

- Separate the quilt top from the border and appliqué the A's to the border. Do not stitch the inner edge of the A's.
- Center the quilt top on the border, as before, and pin them together. Appliqué the quilt top to the border.
- On the wrong side, carefully trim the inner edge of the border frame even with the raw edge of the quilt top.
- Trim the edges of the quilt 3/4" beyond the curved edge of the border A's.
- Finish the quilt according to the *General Directions*, using the 1 1/4" x 44" white bias strips for the binding.

General Directions

About the Patterns

Read through the pattern directions before cutting fabric for the quilt. Pattern directions are presented in step-by-step order.

Fabrics

Yardage is based on 44"-wide fabric with a useable width of 42". I recommend using 100% cotton fabrics. Test all your fabrics to be sure they are colorfast. I suggest washing your fabrics before using them.

Marking Fabric

Always test marking tools for removability, I suggest using silver or white marking tools for dark fabrics and fine line pencils for light fabrics. Always use a sharp pencil and a light touch. Lay a piece of fine-grained sandpaper under the fabric to keep it from slipping while you mark it, if desired.

Templates

Template patterns are full size and, unless otherwise noted, include a 1/4" seam allowance. The solid line is the cutting line and the broken line is the stitching line. Trace pattern pieces on clear plastic. Use a permanent marker to list the pattern letter and grainline, if one is indicated, on each template.

Window Templates

Use a clear plastic "window" to get an idea of how a novelty print will work to best advantage in your quilt. Make the outside dimensions of the window frame the size and shape of the pattern piece or according to the rotary cutting dimensions listed in the pattern, including seam allowances. Mark the inside dimensions the size and shape of the finished quilt pieces. Place the window on the right side of your fabric and adjust as desired. When the fabric in the window appears as you would like it in the finished quilt, simply trace around the outside edge of the template and cut the fabric piece out on the traced line.

Pieced Patterns

For machine piecing, make templates with the seam allowance. Trace around the templates on the right side of the fabric. For hand piecing, make templates without the seam allowance. Trace templates on the wrong side of the fabric, flipping all directional (asymmetrical) templates before tracing, and add a 1/4" seam allowance as you cut the fabric pieces out.

Appliqué Patterns

A seam allowance is not included on appliqué patterns. The solid line is the sewing line. Make a template and lightly trace around it on the right side of the fabric. For needle-turn appliqué, add a 1/8" to 3/16" turn-under allowance when cutting the fabric pieces out. Clip inside curves almost to the pencil line so they will turn under smoothly as you stitch. Do not add a turn-under allowance if you are using fusible appliqué methods.

Needleturn Appliqué

Pin an appliqué piece in position on the background fabric. Using thread to match the appliqué piece, thread a needle with a 15" to 18" length and knot one end. Using your needle, turn under a short section of the allowance on the appliqué piece, and bring the needle from the wrong side of the background fabric up through the fold on the marked line of the appliqué piece. Push the needle through the background fabric, catching a few threads, and come back up through the background fabric and the appliqué piece on the marked line close to the first stitch. Use the point of the needle to turn under and smooth the allowance, and make another stitch in the same way. Continue needleturning and stitching until the piece is completely sewn to the background fabric. To reduce bulk, do not turn under the allowance or stitch where one appliqué piece will be overlapped by another.

Foundation-pieced Patterns

Foundation piecing is a method for making even the smallest blocks with a high degree of accuracy. Foundation patterns are full size and do not include a seam allowance. For each foundation, trace all of the lines and numbers onto paper. You will need one foundation for each block or part of a block as described in the pattern. Cut the foundations out on the outer lines. The inner lines are the stitching lines. The fabric pieces you select do not have to be cut precisely. Be generous when cutting fabric pieces as excess fabric will be trimmed away after sewing. Your goal is to cut a piece that covers the numbered area and extends into surrounding areas after seams are stitched. Generally, fabric pieces should be large enough to extend 1/2" beyond the seamlines on all sides before stitching. For very small sections, or sections without angles, 1/4" may be sufficient. Set the stitch length to 12 stitches per inch.

Place fabric pieces on the unmarked side of the foundation and stitch on the marked side. Center the first piece, right side up, over position 1 on the unmarked side of the foundation. Hold the foundation up to a light to make sure that the raw edges of the fabric extend at least 1/2" beyond the seamline on all sides. Hold this first piece in place with a small dab of glue or a pin, if desired. Place the fabric for position 2 on the first piece, right sides together. Turn the foundation over and sew on the line between 1 and 2, extending the stitching past the beginning and end of the line by a few stitches on both ends. Trim the seam allowance to 1/8". Fold the position 2 piece back, right side up, and press. Continue adding pieces to the foundation in the same manner until all positions are covered and the block is complete. Trim the fabric 1/4" beyond the edges of each foundation.

To avoid disturbing the stitches, do not remove the paper until the blocks have been stitched together and the borders have been added, unless instructed to remove them sooner in the pattern. The pieces will be perforated from the stitching and can be gently pulled free. Use tweezers to carefully remove small sections of the paper, if necessary.